This book belongs to

_____

_____

acacia

alarm clock
a clock that can be set to buzz or ring to wake somebody

angel
a messenger of God

acacia
a small tree or shrub having clusters of small yellow flowers

ambulance
a specially equipped vehicle for carrying the sick or wounded

ant
a tiny black or brown wingless insect.

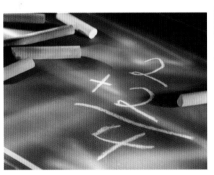

add
to join, unite or put together

anaconda
a large snake that crushes its prey

apartment
a suite of room to live in a large building

aeroplane
a vehicle with wings that flies carrying people

anchor
an object which is used to hold ships from drifting away at the harbour

ape
a big monkey having long arms, broad chest but no tail

apple
a round, red juicy fruit

archery
a sport where shooting is
done with bow and arrow

aster
purplish, blue, pink or white
daisy like flowers

apricot
a small, yellowish-orange fruit

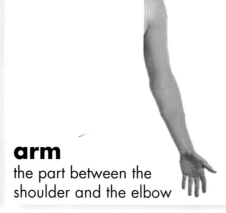

arm
the part between the
shoulder and the elbow

athlete
a person who is an expert
in sport and other physical
exercises

apron
a garment worn over the front
part of the body usually to
protect one's clothes

arrow
a long rod with a pointed tip
and a feathered end

attack
to harm somebody physically

aquarium
a transparent water tank to
keep fishes

artist
a person who makes
drawings and paintings

avocet
a long-legged shorebird with
webbed feet and a slender beak

3

A B C D E F G H I J K L M N O P Q R S T U V W X Y Z

bat ✓
a club used to strike the ball in baseball and in cricket

A metal that is like a cup that keep rings.

bell ✓
a hollow cup like object made of metal which rings when struck

ball ✓
a round toy that bounces

bat ✓
a furry, nocturnal flying animal having wings

bicycle ✓
a vehicle with two wheels which move with pedals

A Colourful Rubber material like filled with air.

balloon
a small, coloured rubber bag filled with air

bear ✓
a large hairy animal with stocky legs, a long snout, and shaggy hair

biscuit ✓
dry and crisp flat eatables which are made from baking

banana
a sweet, curved, yellowish fruit

bee
a four-winged, hairy insect that gather pollen and nectar and live in colonies

bite
to cut with teeth

bike
a lightweight motorcycle

bottle
a glass or plastic container with a narrow neck to keep liquids

bucket
a deep, container used to carry water

blackboard
a large dark board to write with chalk

bowl
a round container

bulb
a type of electric light

boat
a small watercraft which moves by oars, paddles, sails, or an engine

break
to crack or split apart

bus
a rectangular vehicle to carry people

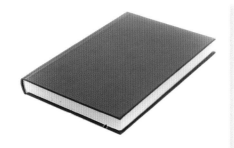

book
a written or printed work on sheets of paper bound together

broccoli
a vegetable which looks like a cauliflower

butterfly
an insect with colourful wings

A B C D E F G H I J K L M N O P Q R S T U V W X Y Z

A
B
C
D
E
F
G
H
I
J
K
L
M
N
O
P
Q
R
S
T
U
V
W
X
Y
Z

car
a vehicle

cat
a small, soft, furry animal

cake
a sweet bread like food made of flour, eggs and sugar

carriage
a vehicle driven by houses

cauliflower
a cream coloured vegetable with a flowery top

camel
an animal which lives in the desert and has long legs

carrot
a fresh orange coloured vegetable

chair
a piece of furniture used for sitting

capsicum
a vegetable

carry
to take from one place to another

chameleon
a lizard which can change colour

A
B
C
D
E
F
G
H
I
J
K
L
M
N
O
P
Q
R
S
T
U
V
W
X
Y
Z

child
a small baby

cock
the male of a chicken

crab
a small animal with four pairs of legs and a pair of pincers

christmas tree
an ever green tree decorated during Christmas

cockatoo
a parrot like bird with high crest

crane
a crane is a lifting machine

computer
an electronic machine which stores a lot of information and does calculation accurately

crocodile
a flesh eating, lizard like animal

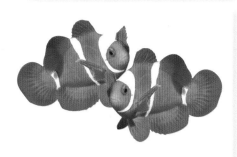

clown fish
a type of fish found in the ocean

cow
the female of a buffalo which gives milk

cup
a small, open container which is usually bowl-shaped and with a handle

A B C D E F G H I J K L M N O P Q R S T U V W X Y Z

deer
a four-footed animal with branched antlers and a white-spotted reddish-brown coat

dish
a round, shallow and concave container made of porcelain or glass for serving food

dalmatian
a breed of dogs with black spots

dentist
a doctor who treats the diseases of teeth

dive
to plunge into water

dam
a barrier built to hold back flowing water

diaper
a sponge like garment worn by people who can't control their urine or stool

dancing
to move the limbs in a rhythmic motion

diary
a notebook for keeping daily written record

doctor
a person who treats us when we are sick

doe
a female dear

door
a wooden, iron or glass
barrier at any entrance

drop
a tiny quantity of any liquid
that is falling, having a pear
shape

dog
a four-footed animal usually
kept as house pets and are
known for their loyalty

dragonfly
a large insect

drum
a cylindrical musical instrument
which is played with sticks

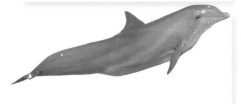

dolphin
is a sea animal that is the
cousin of a whale

drawing
a sketch or a design

duck
a water bird with a broad
blunt bill, short legs and
webbed feet

donkey
a domestic animal of the
horse family which serves as
beasts of burden.

dresser
a chest of drawers generally
with a mirror

duckling
a baby duck

A B C D E F G H I J K L M N O P Q R S T U V W X Y Z

earthen pot
a pot made of mud or clay

eavesdrop
to listen secretly to the private conversation of others

eagle
eagles are large birds of prey with a curved beak

earthworm
a worm with a segmented body that stays in the soil

eclipse
an eclipse occurs when a heavenly body moves into the shade of another body.

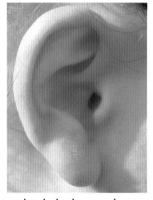

ear
an organ which helps us hear

easel
a three-legged stand to hold an artist's canvas

eel
a snake-like fish with a slender elongated body

earth
the planet on which we live

eat
to put in the mouth, chew and swallow

effort
an attempt to do something

egg
an oval object that is laid by the females of birds

elevator
a box like structure suspended by motor-operated cables for lifting or lowering people or things

engine
a person who designs, builds or maintains machines

egg plant
purple coloured vegetable

emerald
a bright, green, transparent precious stone

eraser
something that erases pencil marks

elbow
the joint between the upper and the lower arm

emu
a large, flightless bird found in Australia

excavator
a huge machine for digging the ground

elephant
a huge plant-eating animal with a trunk, long curved tusks, and large ears

engine
a machine that pulls the train carriages

eye
an organ of the body which helps us to see

A
B
C
D
E
F
G
H
I
J
K
L
M
N
O
P
Q
R
S
T
U
V
W
X
Y
Z

fast
in great speed

fire
something in which objects
burn and turn to ash

face
the front portion of the head

fence
a boundary made of wooden
or metal posts

fire fighter
a person trained to control fire

fan
a machine with rotating
blades to create currents of air

ferries wheel
a grand wheel with passenger
cars

fish
a water animal with scales
on its body

farmhouse
a house situated in a farm

film reel
a frame on which a film tape
is wound

flamingo
a wading bird with pink or
scarlet feathers with a long
neck and legs

float
to be on the surface of a liquid without sinking

fog
a mass of smoke or dust

fork
a spoon with 3 pointed prongs

flood
an overflow of water on dry land

folding chair
a chair that can be folded and made smaller

frame
a solid structure around a photograph

flow
the way liquids move

football
a game played with an inflated leather ball

frog
an amphibian with short legs and a smooth and slimy skin

flower
the part of a plant which has colourful petals

fox
small to medium-sized dog like animals having long, narrow snouts and bushy tails

frying pan
a shallow pan with a handle used for cooking

A
B
C
D
E
F
G
H
I
J
K
L
M
N
O
P
Q
R
S
T
U
V
W
X
Y
Z

A B C D E F **G** H I J K L M N O P Q R S T U V W X Y Z

garden
a piece of land used to grow fruits, flowers and vegetables

gift
an object given to somebody as a sign of love and friendship

gallop
the speedy movement of a horse

gas cylinder
an iron container containing compressed gas

giraffe
the tallest, four-footed living animal

garage
a closed place where motor vehicles are kept

gate
a movable solid structure that swings at the entrance and the exit

girl
a female child or a young woman

garbage bin
a container in which garbage is thrown

gazelle
a small, slender deerlike animal with curved horns

globe
a model of the earth

gloves
a covering for the hand made of wool, cloth or leather

gorilla
the largest and the most powerful of all the apes found mainly in Africa

grater
a utensil with sharp edged holes to grate cheese and vegetables

goat
a domestic animal with curved horns

grapes
a fruit which has green, purple or black berries growing in clusters on a vine

grinder
a machine for crushing and grinding

golf ball
A small, hard ball used is play golf

grass
plants with blade like narrow leaves grown collectively

guitar
a stringed musical instrument

goose
a water bird with webbed feet that resembles a duck

grasshopper
a plant-eating insect with long hind legs

gym
a place for physical training and athletic games and sports

A
B
C
D
E
F
G
H
I
J
K
L
M
N
O
P
Q
R
S
T
U
V
W
X
Y
Z

handkerchief
a square piece of cloth for wiping one's face

hawk
a bird of prey with large wings and a long tail

hair
the fine thread like growth on the skin

hanger
a piece of wood or metal with a hook on top used for hanging clothes

heap
a pile of any substance

hammer
a tool with a metallic head and a wooden handle used for pounding

harbour
a place where ships can anchor

hen
the female bird of the domesticated chicken

hand
the part of the human body attached to the end of the forearm

hat
a covering of the head usually with a brim

helicopter
an aircraft that gets its lift from blades that rotate on its top

heron
a bird with a long neck, long legs and a long, tapering bill

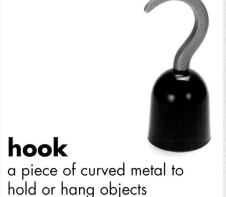

hook
a piece of curved metal to hold or hang objects

hot-air balloon
a large bag filled with hot air which makes it rise

hide
to keep out of sight

hop
to leap on one foot

housefly
a small insect found generally around the house

hill
a raised surface of the earth made naturally

horse
a four-footed animal used mainly for riding and carrying loads

housekeeper
one who manages the household work

home
a place where we live

hot
having high temperature

hovercraft
a vehicle that travels over land and water on cushion of air

A B C D E F G H I J K L M N O P Q R S T U V W X Y Z

ice skates
bladelike metal surface having clamps and straps for fastening it to the shoe used for gliding

igloo
a house made of ice blocks

ice cream
a sweet creamy dessert

ice skating
a skate for skating on ice

iguana
a type of lizard found mostly in central and South America

ice cube
water in a solid form with six equal, square sides

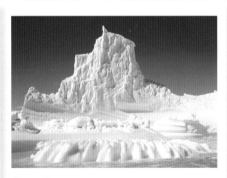

iceberg
a floating mass of ice

iguanodon dinosaur
a plant eating dinosaur with a conical spike on each thumb

ice hockey
a team game played on ice with a curved stick

icicle
a tapering, pointed piece of ice formed by dripping water

impala
a medium sized animal resembling a deer found in Africa

o p q r s t u v w x y z

ivy

A
B
C
D
E
F
G
H
I
J
K
L
M
N
O
P
Q
R
S
T
U
V
W
X
Y
Z

inch tape
a measuring tape

inkpot
a container of ink

iron
a hard silver coloured metal

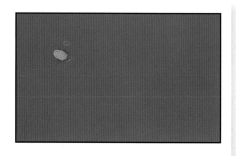

Indian rhino
a large, heavily built plant-eating animal with one or two horns on the nose and thick skin

insect
a small invertebrate animal with six legs, two antennae, and usually having one or two pairs of wings

ironing board
a table with a soft top used for ironing clothes

indigo
deep violet - blue colour

interview
meeting of people face to face for a job or some other pupose

island
a piece of land surrounded by water on all the sides

inject
to put a medicine into the veins

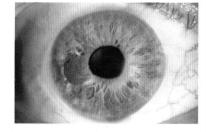

iris
the round, coloured layer surrounding the pupil of the eye

ivy
a climbing vine with a woody stem and evergreen leaves

19

A
B
C
D
E
F
G
H
I
J
K
L
M
N
O
P
Q
R
S
T
U
V
W
X
Y
Z

jade
a hard, precious stone of light bluish green colour

January
the first month of the year

jackal
a medium sized animal which resembles a dog

jaguar
wild cats that live in swamps, deserts and shrubby areas

jar
a container made of glass or stone usually cylindrical in shape

jacket
a short coat usually front open

jail
a place where people committing a serious wrong deed are shut up

jasmine
is a type of shrub and vine with sweet-scented flowers

jackfruit
a large fruit found in Asia

jam
a thick sweet mixture made by boiling fruit with sugar

jay
a noisy bird related to the crow

jeep
a small, sturdy vehicle with four wheels

joey
a baby kangaroo

jug
a container for liquids

jellyfish
is a creature living in the ocean with a body made up of a jellylike substance

jog
to run at a gentle but steady pace

juggle
to continuously toss objects into the air and catch them back while keeping at least one thing in the air at a time

jewellery
ornaments like necklaces, rings or bracelets together

join
to connect

juice
the liquid got from or present in fruits and vegetables

jigsaw puzzle
a puzzle having different shapes sometimes with pictures on them

judge
a person who listens to cases in the court and gives his decision

jump
to rise above the ground with the help of the leg muscles

A
B
C
D
E
F
G
H
I
J
K
L
M
N
O
P
Q
R
S
T
U
V
W
X
Y
Z

A B C D E F G H I J **K** L M N O P Q R S T U V W X Y Z

kennel
a home for a dog

keyboard
the rows of keys of a computer

kangaroo
a large animal found in Australia with a long powerful tail and strong hind limbs

ketchup
a thick sauce made from tomatoes and flavoured with onion and salt

kid
a child

karate
a Japanese style of self defence

kettle
a container with a lid, spout and handle used for boiling water

kimono
a Japanese costume with wide sleeves and a sash

keg
a small barrel like container

key
something that is used to open locks

king
a ruler of a state or kingdom

king cobra
the most poisonous snake in the world

kite
a toy which flies and has a thin frame with some material stretched over it

knot
a lump in a cord formed by passing the loose end through a loop

kingfisher
an insect eating bird with a long, stout bill and a crest

kite
a long-winged bird of prey with a forked tail

koala
a grey coloured hairy animal which lives on trees in Australia

kiss
to touch lightly with the lips

kiwi
a flightless, tailless New Zealand bird with hair-like feathers

krill
a small sea creature like the shrimp

kitchen
the room where one cooks food

knife
a sharp blade with a pointed edge used for chopping

kung fu
a Chinese martial art

A
B
C
D
E
F
G
H
I
J
K
L
M
N
O
P
Q
R
S
T
U
V
W
X
Y
Z

A
B
C
D
E
F
G
H
I
J
K
L
M
N
O
P
Q
R
S
T
U
V
W
X
Y
Z

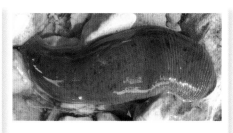

lark
a songbird with brown streaky feathers

leech
a type of worm

labrador
a breed of dog with a black or yellow coat used as a guide

laugh
to express joy with an audible sound from the lungs

lemon
a small, round, pale yellow citrus fruit

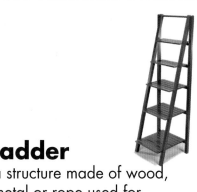

ladder
a structure made of wood, metal or rope used for climbing up or down

leaf
a part of the plant that grows from the stem and are usually flat

leopard
a large ferocious cat usually having a tawny coat spotted with black

ladybug
a small insect with a domed back, red coloured skin with black spots

leap
jump or spring a long way

letter box
a box where letters are put when delivered

lick
to pass the tongue over something

llama
an animal which looks like a camel and is used as a beast of burden

log
a portion of the trunk of a tree

lion
a large, powerful animal with a shaggy mane and a tufted tail

loaf
a single piece of bread

lollypop
a piece of candy fixed at the tip of a small stick

listen
to make an effort to hear something

lobster
edible sea creature, stalk-eyed having large pincers on the first pair of legs

lotus
water plant with large, water lily-like flowers

lizard
a scaly reptile having an elongated body, a tapering tail and two pairs of legs

lock
an object that helps to close a door or the lid of a container

lychee
a small, oval shaped fruit with a red outer cover and a sweet pulp inside

A
B
C
D
E
F
G
H
I
J
K
L
M
N
O
P
Q
R
S
T
U
V
W
X
Y
Z

map
a flat diagram of an area of land or sea

marry
to join as husband and wife

machine
an object which is driven by power and used to do some work

maple tree
a type of tree

mastiff
a large dog of a strong breed with drooping ears and hanging lips

man
an adult human male

march
the third month of the year

mat
a piece of fabric made of rushes or straw to cover the floor

mango
a fleshy, sweet, oval, yellowish-red fruit

market
a place full of shops where people buy and sell things

matchbox
a small box holding matchsticks

May
the fifth month of the year

monitor
a part of the computer which acts like a screen

motorboat
a small boat propelled by an engine or motor

melt
to change from the solid to liquid state

monkey
a small to medium-sized animal having a long tail and which lives on trees

mouse
a small palm sized animal with tiny ears and a long tail

milk
a white liquid produced by mothers to feed their babies

moon
the silvery celestial body seen in the night sky

mud
wet, soft, sticky soil

mirror
a smooth , shiny surface that reflects the images of objects

mother
a woman who has given birth to a child

mug
a drinking cup made of metal or earthenware

A B C D E F G H I J K L M N O P Q R S T U V W X Y Z

A B C D E F G H I J K L M N O P Q R S T U V W X Y Z

nail polish
a colour applied on the nails for its beautification

narrow
not having much space

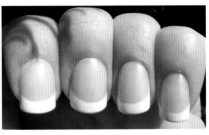

nail
a part of the body which grows out from the tips of the fingers

name plate
a metallic or wooden plate with name or names written

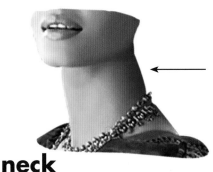

narwhal
a medium sized toothed whale

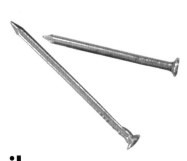

nail
a small metal spike with a broad, flat head

nap
a short sleep

neck
the part of the body which joins the head to the body

nail brush
a small nail brush for cleaning nails

napkin
a small piece of cloth or paper used while eating for wiping the fingers or the mouth

necklace
a piece of ornament worn around the neck

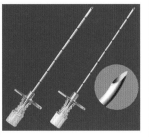

needle
a thin, piece of steel with a hole on one side to put a thread with a pointed end

newt
an amphibian with an elongated body

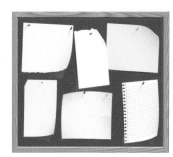

notice board
a board where information is put up for all

nest
a home of the birds

night
the time from sunset to sunrise

78

number
a quantity or value expressed by a symbol or figure

net
a fabric made from string or cord loosely knotted or woven used to trap birds and fishes

nipple
a small object made of rubber fixed on a baby's nursing bottle used to suck

nun
a religious lady who lives under the vows of poverty and chastity

newspaper
a published paper with news which comes out daily or weekly

nose
a part of the human face used for smelling

nurse
a person trained to take care of the sick and the injured

A
B
C
D
E
F
G
H
I
J
K
L
M
N
O
P
Q
R
S
T
U
V
W
X
Y
Z

ocean
a vast body of water

officer
a person appointed to a position of authority

oak tree
a big hardwood tree

octagon
a figure with eight sides

oars
a wooden pole with a flat blade at one end used to row a boat

octopus
a sea creature with four pairs of arms

ogre
an ugly, man-eating monster found in fairy tales

oats
a cereal

office
a place where people work to earn a salary

ointment
a thick, creamy substance with healing properties

olive
a small oval fruit with a hard seed and bitter flesh

orangutan
a great ape with shaggy, reddish-brown hair and very long arms

otter
a fish eating animal that lives partly on land and partly on water

omelette
beaten eggs cooked as a pancake

orchard
a place where fruit trees are grown

oven
a device in which food is cooked or baked

onion
a vegetable that grows underground

orchestra
a group of people playing various instruments

owl
a nightly bird with large eyes and a hooked beak

orange
a sweet, round, juicy orange coloured citrus fruit

ostrich
the largest living bird

oyster
an edible, sea creature

A
B
C
D
E
F
G
H
I
J
K
L
M
N
O
P
Q
R
S
T
U
V
W
X
Y
Z

31

A
B
C
D
E
F
G
H
I
J
K
L
M
N
O
P
Q
R
S
T
U
V
W
X
Y
Z

parachute
an umbrella shaped cloth which fills with air and helps heavy objects or people to come down slowly from an aeroplane

peep
to see through a small opening or from a place of hiding

painter
a man who paints houses and walls

parrot
birds which are mostly green in colour with a curved beak and clawed feet

pen
an instrument for writing with ink

painting
a painted picture

pea
a climbing plant with green seedpods

pencil
a thin, wooden, rod shaped object used for writing

paper
thin sheets made from the pulp of wood

peacock
a bird with long, brightly coloured tail feathers

penguin
a flightless black and white seabird found in the southern hemisphere

photograph
a picture taken by a camera

pilot
a person who drives an aeroplane

play
to take part in games and sports

piano
a large musical instrument which plays when the keys are pressed by hammers

pink
a colour

pull
to exert force on something so that it is drawn towards ones' self

pie
a baked dish having either an under crust, an upper crust, or both

plant
a young tree

pump
something that uses suction or pressure to raise or move liquids or gases

pig
a small, domesticated animal with a thin layer of hair and a flat snout

platypus
a small mammal with webbed feet and a beaver like tail

punch
to strike with the fist

A B C D E F G H I J K L M N O P Q R S T U V W X Y Z

33

A B C D E F G H I J K L M N O P Q R S T U V W X Y Z

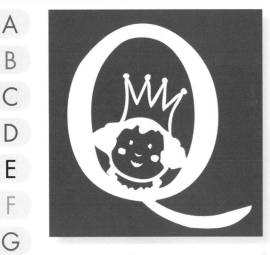

queen
wife of a king

quiet
silent, calm

quail
a small short-tailed bird, with brown feathers

question mark
a symbol put at the end of the questions

quill
tail feather of a bird

quarrel
an argument

quetzal
a bird with green feathers, red underpants and a crest

quilt
a bedcover filled with cotton or wool

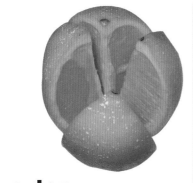

quarter
one part out of four parts

queue
a line of people and vehicles awaiting their turn

quiver
a case where arrows are kept

R

radish
a small, pungent, root of a plant that is eaten raw

rainbow
an arc containing seven colours which appears in the sky after a shower of rain

rabbit
a burrowing, furry, plant-eating animal with long ears

raft
a flat, floating structure made of logs used as a boat

rake
a tool used for gathering loose grass

race
a competition of speed in running, riding or driving

rain
water falling in drops from the sky to the earth

ram
a male sheep

radio
an instrument from which we hear programmes through electromagnectic waves

raincoat
a waterproof coat worn in the rain to protect ourselves

run
to move swiftly

A
B
C
D
E
F
G
H
I
J
K
L
M
N
O
P
Q
R
S
T
U
V
W
X
Y
Z

raspberry
a soft reddish edible fruit

reindeer
a type of deer

ring
an ornament worn on the fingers

rat
a palm-sized animal with a long tail known as a pest

rhinoceros
a large, heavy, thick-skinned, plant-eating animal

river
a large stream of water

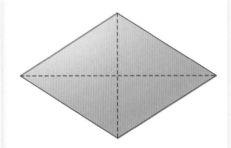

reading
to read something from a book or a reading material

rhombus
a type of shape

road
a way for travellers

rectangle
a shape with opposite sides equal

ribbon
a narrow strip of silk or nylon used for tying

road roller
a vehicle with a heavy roller used for making roads

robin
a small European songbird

rooster
a male chicken

row
to move a boat with the help of oars

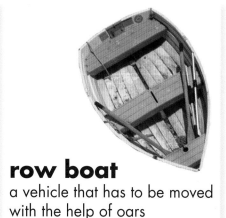

rocket
a spacecraft

roots
the part of the plant that is generally below the ground

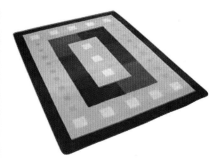

row boat
a vehicle that has to be moved with the help of oars

roller coaster
an amusement ride

rope
a thick, strong cord

rug
a woven fabric used to cover the floor

roof
the upper covering of houses or vehicles

rose
a flower with a pleasant scent

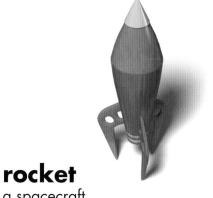

rye
cereal plant

A B C D E F G H I J K L M N O P Q R S T U V W X Y Z

A
B
C
D
E
F
G
H
I
J
K
L
M
N
O
P
Q
R
S
T
U
V
W
X
Y
Z

scorpion
a creature with pincers and a poisonous sting at the end of its tail

shoes
an outer covering for the human foot made of leather or canvas

salt
a white crystalline substance which is used in cooking to add taste

screw
a device for fastening things

snail
a small creature with a shell which lives on land and water

scissors
an instrument for cutting

sheep
a four-footed domestic animal which gives us wool

snake
a long, thin crawling reptile

scooter
a vehicle having two wheels and a low, narrow foot board.

ship
a vehicle for travelling on oceans and seas driven by engine

soap
a substance used with water for washing or cleaning

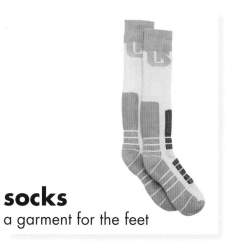

socks
a garment for the feet

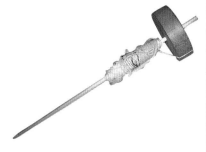

spindle
a slender rod or pin used in spinning

sugar
a sweet crystalline substance used to sweeten food and drinks

sparrow
a tiny, brown bird found in Europe, Asia and Africa

spoon
a utensil used for picking up food and stirring

sun
central star of the solar system

spider
an insect that spins a web and has eight legs

starfish
a sea creature in the shape of a star

sunflower
large, yellow, daisy like flowers

spinach
a green leafy vegetable

strawberry
a small, red fleshy fruit

swan
a large water bird with a long neck and white feathers

table

A B C D E F G H I J K L M N O P Q R S **T** U V W X Y Z

tea
a hot drink that is made by boiling the dried leaves of a tea plant

telescope
an instrument which makes distant objects appear nearer

table
a piece of furniture having a flat, horizontal top and four legs

teach
to give lessons

tent
a portable shelter made of canvas

tap
an object for starting or stopping the flow of a liquid

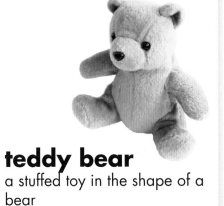

teddy bear
a stuffed toy in the shape of a bear

thermometer
an instrument for measuring the temperature of our body

tarantula
hairy spiders with a poisonous bite

telephone
an instrument through which one can talk to people far away

tiger
a large fierce Asian cat having a brownish-yellow coat and black stripes

tin
an airtight container used for preserving food

tortoise
a slow moving, plant eating reptile with a shell on its back

truck
a vehicle for carrying loads

tip
the pointed or rounded extreme end of something that is tapering

towel
a piece of absorbent cloth used while bathing

t-shirt
a collarless shirt made of cotton

toad
an amphibian with a rough, warty skin

tractor
a powerful vehicle used for pulling farm machinery

tulip
a plant with large trumpet-shaped flowers

tomato
A round, red coloured citrus fruit

train
a series of railway carriages or wagons pulled by an engine

turtle
animals that live in water with a toothless beak and a soft body hidden within a hard shell

A B C D E F G H I J K L M N O P Q R S T **U** V W X Y Z

unclean
untidy, not clean

unicycle
a one-wheeled vehicle

umbrella
a shade made of cloth stretched over a folding frame used for protection against the rain or sun

under
beneath something

uniform
the special clothing worn by members of the same organization or a school

umpire
an official who administers the rules in a team sports

unequal
not equal

university
an educational institution giving higher education

uncle
the brother of one's father or mother

unhappy
not having joy

urn
a tall, rounded vase

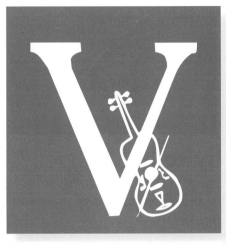

velvet
a closely woven silk material

violet
a colour

valley
a stretch of low land lying between hills or mountains

vest
a short, tight-fitting, sleeveless garment worn, especially under a suit coat

violin
a stringed instrument played with a bow

van
a closed truck

villa
a large country house

volcano
a mountain or hill through which rock fragments, hot vapour and gas comes out from the earth's crust

vegetable
a plant or part of a plant used as food

vinegar
a sour tasting liquid

vulture
a large bird of prey

A
B
C
D
E
F
G
H
I
J
K
L
M
N
O
P
Q
R
S
T
U
V
W
X
Y
Z

43

A
B
C
D
E
F
G
H
I
J
K
L
M
N
O
P
Q
R
S
T
U
V
W
X
Y
Z

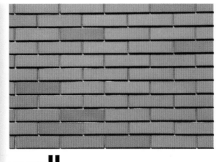

wall
an upright structure of wood, stone, brick made to enclose

whale
a very large sea animal with a blowhole on top of the head for breathing

wagon
a horse-drawn vehicle, used for transporting goods

wallet
a pocket-sized, folding holder for money

wolf
a carnivorous animal that lives and hunts in packs

waist
the part of the body between the ribs and the hips

walrus
a large animal with two tusks pointing downwards

woodpecker
a bird with a strong beak used for pecking at tree trunks to find insects

walk
to go along or move about on foot

wasp
a winged insect which has a black and yellow striped body

worm
a creeping or burrowing insect having a long slender soft body and no limbs

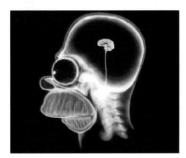

x-ray film
a photograph of the internal structure of an object

xylophone
a musical instrument

A
B
C
D
E
F
G
H
I
J
K
L
M
N
O
P
Q
R
S
T
U
V
W
X
Y
Z

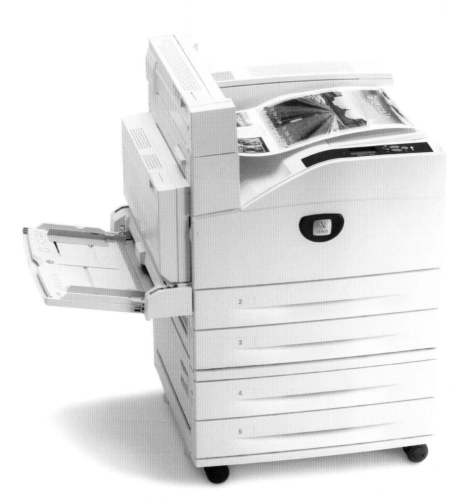

xerox machine
a machine that makes copies of printed material

A
B
C
D
E
F
G
H
I
J
K
L
M
N
O
P
Q
R
S
T
U
V
W
X
Y
Z

yawn
to open the mouth wide and breathe in deeply as a result of weariness

yoga
a Hindu spiritual branch of learning which teaches methods to improve the body and the mind

yacht
a medium-sized sailing boat having equipments for cruising or racing

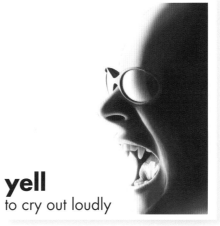

yell
to cry out loudly

yogurt
a semi-solid slightly sour food prepared from fermented milk by added bacteria

yak
a large ox with shaggy hair and large horns used in Tibet

yellow
a colour

yolk
the yellow internal part of a bird's egg

yarn
thread used for knitting, weaving, or sewing

yellow bird
a tiny yellow coloured bird

yo-yo
a toy with two joined discs

zero
a numerical symbol that
denotes no value

zip
something that joins two
adjoining edges of a material

zebra
a horse like animal with black
and white stripes

zigzag
a pattern having abrupt
alternate right and left turns

zinnia
a plant known for its bright showy flowers

zoo
a place where wild animals
are kept for people to see

A
B
C
D
E
F
G
H
I
J
K
L
M
N
O
P
Q
R
S
T
U
V
W
X
Y
Z

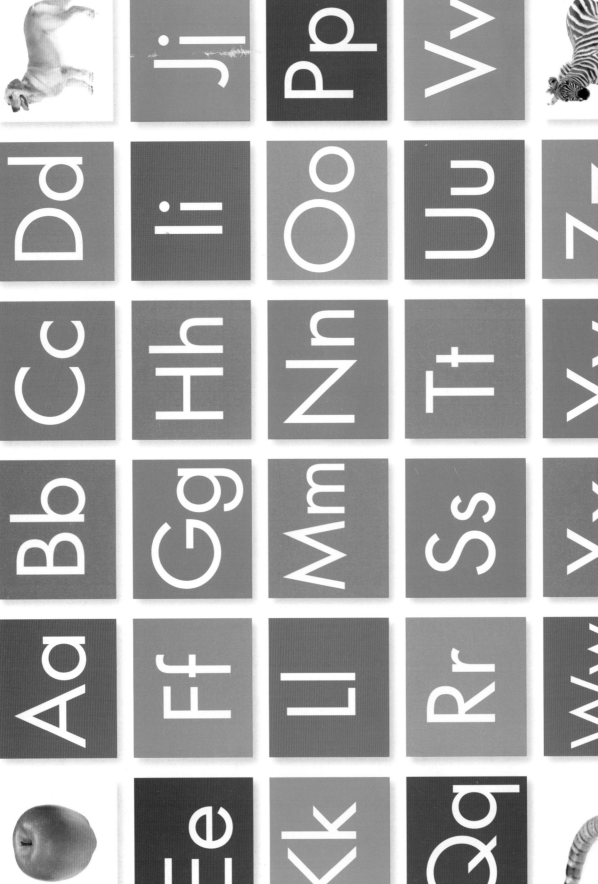